POETRY
— now —

EACH AND EVERY MOMENT

Edited by

Heather Killingray

First published in Great Britain in 2000 by
POETRY NOW
Remus House,
Coltsfoot Drive,
Woodston,
Peterborough, PE2 9JX
Telephone (01733) 898101
Fax (01733) 313524

HB ISBN 0 75430 961 4
SB ISBN 0 75430 962 2

FOREWORD

Although we are a nation of poets we are accused of not reading poetry, or buying poetry books. After many years of listening to the incessant gripes of poetry publishers, I can only assume that the books they publish, in general, are books that most people do not want to read.

Poetry should not be obscure, introverted, and as cryptic as a crossword puzzle: it is the poet's duty to reach out and embrace the world.

The world owes the poet nothing and we should not be expected to dig and delve into a rambling discourse searching for some inner meaning.

The reason we write poetry (and almost all of us do) is because we want to communicate: an ideal; an idea; or a specific feeling. Poetry is as essential in communication, as a letter; a radio; a telephone, and the main criterion for selecting the poems in this anthology is very simple: they communicate.

CONTENTS

INTO THE EMPTINESS

The bare root of Dorothy Perkins you gave me
I planted ten years ago under the pine trees
that died so I thought as it had to
has with these spectacular rains grown again.

My mare moves away from my right leg onto her
into the emptiness my left leg makes as I take it off her
we traverse the arena going into the wall and off the wall.
It's as simple as that.

Because you weren't here I started and finished without you.
Howling to fall off the edge of the world
I looked into my uncorrupt face and saw myself nameless.

Jennifer Compton

THE BECKONING WAVE

She came, we met, bear with me yet,
We walked the sands, how we laughed,
Watched sun's demise, then moon's white shaft,
Across the sea, so calm, so vast.

From morning tide, till shadows cast,
All magic month I held her fast,
Now she has gone and left me here
To promenade the lonely pier.

City life, the clubs, the trendy pack,
These things combined, lured her back,
This above all things I fear
Life without one who was most dear.

Now where we walked hand in hand,
There's just my footprints in the sand,
One day when I'm feeling brave
They will lead to Beckoning Wave.

G Nicklin

MY MEMORIES OF

(We'll meet again some day - love, a cousin)

A girl cocooned in a needless shell of a body
She was cruelly dealt a suffering blow
With no easy life to meander and flow

We can never imagine
The depth of her pain
No bathing in sunshine
Or dancing in rain

No breath on the window
To wipe for a view
Her tormented days
Are thankfully through

The sun will dawn
On her life here no more
So now as she passes
Through heaven's grand door

Farewell to Julie
Another princess
And in God's holy kingdom
She'll peacefully rest.

A Cartlidge

BLOWN AWAY

What were you thinking
When you walked away from me
Were you on some strange high
That made you feel
As though you were king
And you could do it by yourself.

You were unable to talk
Your mind has been blown away
Far away
Never to be recovered
Because of the high
That you want more than me.

Are you alive under there anymore
Or are you a shell
A person on the outside
Empty on the inside
Incapable of feeling anything
Except for the high.

Rebecca Moorhouse (17)

ALL ALONE

Alone
Confined into one small space
Decor is what you decided
Posters showing your taste
Accessorised with things of your own
Some may be personal
Some may be presents
Some may be designer
Some may be practical
But whatever they are, they're yours
All yours in a space you call your own
A space where you can do what you please
And where is this place you ask
It's wherever you want it to be.

Samantha McInnes (13)

THE LADY ON THE BEACH

The dolphins were playing and leaping for joy
As I ran on the pale golden beach.
I was anxious to join in the pleasure they gave
And the lessons to humans they teach

A lady approached, on her way from the sea,
A stranger she was, dressed in black,
With a hat made of straw, a fine silken scarf,
And a shimmer of gold at her neck.

We were destined to meet on that hot foreign beach
As we stared out to sea for a while.
She was dying, she said, though she did not know when
And each day was a bonus, till then.

Her home, in Ohio, was distant for sure
And soon she would drive through the night
To the family she loved and a future unknown
Where she'd tried to do everything right.

We spoke of our faith and the comfort it gave
And I treasure our meeting that day
There was so much to say, by the Mexican Bay,
As the dolphins continued to frolic and play.

The world holds such wonder, enjoyment, and strife
And we don't always measure the true wealth of life
But the meeting with Beth on that beach far away
Will be in my heart to my last living day.

Brenda Robinson

UNTITLED

Freezing rain pours down
from grey skies on the gathering,
bitter-sweet with overuse
of the word 'historic'.
The dawning of a new era
the building of a new road.
A road for decades, dark-strewn,
with ancient suspicions.
A shadow hangs,
still to be lightened.
With the children,
their children's children,
hope still lies.
For without hope,
we may see a long way,
but not as far as that.

Jim Fraser

WHERE ARE YOU GOING?

Where are you going
In such a hurry
All wrapped up in
Your world of worry
All stressed and strained
And struggling strife
You twist and turn
The steely knife
Where are you going
In such a frazzle
All mobile phone
And razzle, dazzle
Too fast to live
Too slow to see
The price of
Immortality
Where are you going
In such a flurry
All rat ta tat
And scat and scurry
Afraid to smile
And show your hand
All 'savoir faire'
And sinking sand
Where are you going
In such a muddle
All traffic jam
And fuddy duddle
All caught up in
A corporate dream
Of nearly men
That might have been

Rod Trott

VAUXHALL ROYALE

Where elegance and grandeur dwell
The Royale though old, still casts a spell,
A sound like thunder from within,
Propels this vehicle like the wind,
And thus its purpose is decreed,
To give its owner torque and speed,
A thousand built but few remain,
To carry this mark to greater fame.

David A Bray

OFF-LINE

'Are you on line?' I was asked yesterday.
'Well I think I am.' I said.
'I felt a bit dizzy when I first woke up,
But I improved once I'd got out of bed.'
'No. Are you on line?' she asked once again.
'Are you on the net?'
And here she became quite aggressive.
Her expression was cold and all set.
'No I am not on the net.' I answered.
'And what's more I'm not likely to be.
I've barely just mastered the video,
So the network's a mystery to me
I don't want to go shopping with old Dot Com
I don't want to visit the web.
Nor surf the network with a little grey mouse.
Just leave me alone instead.
To Hell with the scanners and modem and screen.
To Hell with the e-mail too.
And as for that WWW dot,
Well you know what you can do.'

Betty Pearson

LIFE'S 'PATCHWORK'

Cobwebs, soft as gossamer
Fragile and woven like dreams
That needs tender understanding
Life and loves
Are never what they seem
Woven mysteries of life
Like a 'silent night'.
We must weave out lives
Like a spinning wheel   .
Spin a pattern
In quite thoughts
So our lives
Be enriched
With family, friends,
And people we meet   ,
Along life's way.

Margaret Parnell

THE FINAL INDIGNATION

You cannot hold your job with us,
You have no qualification,
Why don't you leave without a fuss,
The final indignation!

You've been around a very long time,
Each job you gladly sorted,
But as was said in your nursery rhyme,
It's time you had departed!

We will not talk of cabbages,
Such as things as kings do often,
Far less corporate ravages;
The chairman will not soften!

Tom Ritchie

FROM THE HEART

The tongue is very changeable -
It's courteous and it's kind.
But it can be spiteful
If bad thoughts are in one's mind.

A spark can cause a fire
To rage and to destroy
And so a word called 'gossip'
Is spoken to annoy.

Sometimes this is in innocence -
Remarks with not much thought -
Starting out in childhood
And the way that we are taught.

The tongue can be a source of joy
Where peace can be one's goal -
And friendship built on mutual trust
Can heal a hurting soul.

Before we speak - engage our brain
To those we are addressing.
The tongue we have - for good or bad
Can be - or not - a blessing.

Pat Melbourn

LAST DAY

There's no turning back
For Johnny Mac
As he ponders through his mind
O' what can I do
My life's been hard
I've earned my crust
It's the only thing I've had to do
They say the old pit life is through
It's time to call it a day
As pits are closing day by day

Life's been hard
I've sweated blood
But the manager shouts
Get out into the fresh air
Your lungs will be clear
Yes, you may have the odd cough and flu
You'll live a long, long life
You'll get your coal and your blocks
For the rest of your life

But as time passed
His last was his last
Work became harder throughout the day
He remembers as from a boy workmates become friends
Hell has been like life deep underground
My best friends being my old shovel and pick
As blast after blast seams fell away and the barrier coal fell
With big large lumps and watery mud
My body all wet and tired, my bones ache and creak
The dust rises from my feet to my face
As our lamps light up our places

As a job well done we walk to the cage
Where our old friend the On's man
Greets us from the cage as upwards we go to the pit face
As we hit the surface the sun dazzles us with its glare
Our bodies all tired and worn we walk to the baths
Where soap and water wash away the day's grain, as boy became man
As we sing songs of Cwm Rhondda tears run down my face
My time has been hard but even harder today
As my goodbyes are said for the last time
On this my last day

Tony Jones

SEND OFF A LETTER

What makes the loudest noise?
The sound of battle
Or the beating heart
Of one of our brave soldier boys
All he hears is his heart beating loud
Like thunder above a storm cloud
He thinks of his mother
Or maybe his wife or sweetheart
While waiting for the battle to start
His heart beats faster, louder too
As he goes over the top
To fight for me and you,
Loud his heart beats, faster too,
Then it stops!
Now give him a medal
For being so brave
Then put his young body
In an old soldier's grave.
Now send off your letter
To his mother or wife
And say he fought bravely
But a bullet took his life
Now remember this young soldier
And what he and others went through
To give a free country
For me and for you.

Joseph Bell

WHEN THE MARRIAGE WAS BLESSED

Church bells were chiming out, the day the marriage was blessed
The birds were singing merrily, to chirp their very best
The sun was shining brightly, the clouds had drifted away
When Esther and Paul went through the ceremony, on a special day

An organ was playing in the background, 'twas such a harmony
Hymns were sang with ecstasy, sounding a sweet melody
The church was full with people, while music filled the place
The two in love stood hand in hand, so proud and full of grace

The vows were pronounced by the pastor, and blessed by God above
While, Paul was looking distinguished, his eyes so full of love
Esther was looking radiant, where God's light shone around
As the pastor was praying for the both, on sacred, holy ground

More prayers were rising to God, by leaders and the elders
The two were blessed again, clinging to each other
Magic moments were shared, as they stole a loving kiss
Knowing heavenly love was within, and life ahead of bliss

While signing the register, their parents stood proudly near
Still, music was sounding softly, so wonderful and clear
Happiness was there between them, like a lovely dream come true
Even when photographs were taken, in the Garden's picturesque

Till, time was drawing nigh, for the traditional celebration
Drinks and food was served my waiters, at the special occasion
One special guest was invited throughout, even to wine and dine
The good spirit of Jesus was present, truly the holy divine

When the feasting was over, they danced throughout the night
Jesus joined the merriment, and shone His dazzling light
God made the marriage blessing possible, for Esther and for Paul
And gave the day so much sunshine, till evening did befall

Jean P McGovern

NOT ALL PAIN IS GAIN

It's fifty-five years since I buried your remains,
That were picked from the far foreign field,
In all of those years I have woken each morn,
And expected that my wounds would heal.
But I never stopped wanting that man that I sent,
Even though you were long gone from me,
I somehow believed that if I cried hard enough,
Then death would somehow set you free.

It's fifty-five days since you took leave of us,
Now your boy has a bedwetter's trait,
I lie through my teeth to your daughter,
So that she won't be embittered by hate.
I had rested my heart on your love for me,
I feel stupid, naive and alone,
I'm caught between feelings of murdering you,
And hopes that you'll just come back home.

This fifty-fifth year will suffice I think,
I am shrunken and hairless and gaunt.
With no humour with which to ensnare me some sex,
No physical prowess to flaunt.
My morphine is all that I court,
When agony creeps up like some thief,
Each spasm reminds me of this,
That my death will be my relief.

Five fifty-five on a Friday,
Surely dying can't be any worse,
Can next week's work at the office,
Be worse than a ride in a hearse.
The days of this life tick away,
Each one snatched from my arms,
Almost unnoticed their preciousness,
Oblivious I dwell, unalarmed.

Ray Burton

THE LONELINESS OF A WINTER'S EVENING

Just sitting here, I'm nearly eighty-two,
Yes, sitting here just wondering what I should do,
I'm rather limited you see, because of my aches and pains,
As I've lost all confidence in those treatment tales,

Shadows now appear to creep around my room,
Just adding to this nightly gloom,
Not to forget, also that silence will set in soon,
My fire I see needs my attention,
The embers have now lost their glow,
And as I approach my window to close my curtains
I see that there's been a little snow.

This time of the year everything looks so very glum,
I'm afraid to face whatever there is to come,
Those winter evenings, when the winds begin to whine,
I turn my head towards my clock,
Just then it began to chime,

When you get old you must confess,
Life in many ways brings on the stress,
Your habits get somewhat bored,
With nothing to look forward to,
My clock now tells me that it's gone nine,
Which to me, it's getting near my bed time,
Goodnight, is about all I can further say,
Trusting to God,
That he brings me another day.

D Gorton

THE GOVERNMENT'S LOGIC!

The government! Where do they get their logic?
For I find their reasoning, simply tragic.
The addict they say . . . give more cash,
Help them to buy . . . their little stash.
And as for the poor alcoholics?
Give them more for their gin and tonics.

But those habits? They are self-induced,
Yet their addictions . . . are excused.
Whilst the smoker the hospitals don't want to treat,
They'd rather see us die upon the street.
Where do they think the money comes from?
To enable them their tasks to perform?

The tax for the smoker rises higher and higher,
Hoping tobacconists won't find a buyer.
They want us to stop our only pleasure,
Leave us just a memory to treasure.
The tax from our cigarettes fill their coffers,
For from their salaries we hear no offers.

No more cigarette tax for the NHS!
'Twill be the turn of the motorist then I guess!

M Muirhead

THE TWO DOLPHINS

Long ago, according to legend,
There were two dolphins spotted by fishermen.
One swam from the west, the other from the east.
Then they met each other for the very first time.
The male circled the female . . .
Then she followed his example . . .
Then they circled together . . .
The fishermen watched in wonder and smiled.
Yet this went on the whole day long . . .
The fishermen scratched their heads at the spectacle.
'It must be love!' they agreed.
'But they haven't eaten anything!' said a little boy.
'May I swim over to them with some fish?' he asked.
'Certainly, lad! Go ahead! Give them the strength in their courtship!'
So off the boy went with some fish for the dolphins . . .
The two dolphins stopped and waited for him.
He gave them some fish and they ate them gladly.
Then, to show their appreciation, they danced for him . . .
This thrilled him so much he wept for joy . . .
He waved to them as they swam away side-by-side.
It was a wondrous day for the dolphins . . .
For not only had they found love but friendship as well . . .
And in this world, it doesn't get much better than that . . .
No matter who you are . . .

Denis Martindale

ENDANGERED SPECIES

Our old folk went through two huge wars
but, suffer more at home,
they're mugged which means robbed in new
speak of which our government owns a great tome.

Who cares if there's glass in our windows
for people over fifty years,
the council will back little Johnny who
they think will vote labour dears.

Which means lots of them have forgotten
you don't get to vote from a cell,
but, when you look into those blank eyes
you know he'll be there for a spell.

Once we spent money on people who cared
and worked hard at good schools,
now it all goes on some strange creatures
and it's man after man that he drools.

Parents do not have a framework where
children learn there is a boss,
by the time they learn that there is one
they're in Borstal mourning their loss.

The old folk with brains are resented
instead of being listened to keen,
so, all of their great fund of knowledge
is lost as if it had not been.

While people find relatives dead and
think that someone should be charged,
murderers at play just drive their cars
away, shoot their drugs and have photos enlarged.

We now need an army at home to try
and take care of our own,
for if we do not care, wake up and do our share,
civilisation will be quite unknown.

Jean Paisley

THE AFRICAN DILEMMA

Over all the African nations
   the troubles never cease
Which is to do with their past history
   and where there never will be peace

The whites came with their bibles
   the blacks then owned the land
now it's the blacks who have the bible
   whilst the whites are in command

With the blacks being ignorant of business
   and with no real education
the whites stole from them their birthright
   with no signs of restoration

Now with better education
   the blacks can see their loss
and today they try to break the chains
   where the whites are always boss

So with those troubling aspects
   taking place on Africa's shore
let's hope we don't have lots of killing
   to make up for those old sores.

Lachlan Taylor

GIRLS ON BOYS

Clinically defined
a question to be answered,
smiles so bright, or foggy and implanted,
they strike you with a lance or a blunt spade.

Steady, uneven, slow, fast,
here, there, somewhere, someone.

Without them there is nothing,
with them can come nothing.
One man, one thought,
cupid was a woman.

Every other person is:
calm rash, funny, boring.

An understanding is impossible,
one can never see clearly through the glass.

Being one with the glass,
to fill it with the liquid of your heart,
will bring a state where you'll never be apart -
from the one who is:
strong, weak, gentle, harsh.

Gemma Keyte (18)

WE LIVE WITHIN

In moments of meditation
A pause for circumspection
May lead to illumination -
A thought, an idea, an image
May appear and presage
A towering experience,
A discovery of great importance
To your future way
Of discovering life, the world, the day.
Do not ignore the premonition,
The intuition, the inspiration,
But unfold, with all imagination,
The path you are destined to follow.
The truth, becoming clear, is not hollow.
By looking into the mind,
Pure enlightenment we find.

David W Hill

Snowdrop

Tender flower
Humble
Chaste
Artistry
With
Slender grace

Irene Gunnion

BEFORE YOUR EYES

I thirst to drink that passion from your lips
And hunger to taste the sweetness of your desire
I yearn to feel the spark of fingertips
And then the burning of your loving fire

I crave that tingle running down my spine
And long to hear you whispering my name
I fantasise that you may yet be mine
Before your eyes, my love, I have no shame.

Kim Montia

WHY?

Why did I move to America all those years ago?
I was young and in love and foolish. How was I to know?
Who will look after my parents? They are getting older now.
My brother has moved here also. My guilt causes row after row
with my conscience. Would I be able to move back?
What about my husband and family? In the U.K. they would feel the
lack of the U.S. members of the family tree.
After twenty years, will the homesickness never go?
Could I live there again? I don't really know.
Can I ever be truly happy again? I feel so torn every day.
Always thinking of other things as I watch my children play.
Here I have a big house, big car but I might as well be living on Mars.
Feeling very mortal now. What will I decide?
Is there no easy answer to where I will reside?
As usual, I will put my thoughts on hold.
Everyday life will encroach until I am old
and it's too late.

Christine Walker

GODS

Did one God conceive mankind
or mankind create the Gods
like the blind precede the blind
as each human homeward plods

on his pilgrim way to Allah
or on horseback to Valhalla

Once upon a time there were
many Gods and Goddesses
holding humankind in fear
by sending them on odysseys.

Most Gods live in heaven above
making war or making love

Three to settle some dispute
gave an apple to a boy
she to whom he gave the fruit
sent the thousand ships to Troy

Lancashire and Yorkshire chose
to pick a quarrel for a rose

East met West in eight crusades
fighting for the Holy Lands
unremembered for decades
buried under desert sands

Arabs and Israelis now
still pursue the ancient row

India threatens Pakistan
Pakistan demands Kashmir
Once again bewildered man
begs the Gods to interfere

Whatever happened to that war
to end all wars forever more

Armageddon looms in sight
mobilising everyone
into that long last goodnight
But when all is said and done

were there any Gods before
the advent of the dinosaur?

James Hodgson

ANGELA
(Dedicated to Angela M Rafferty)

You are on my mind and in my dreams,
Please, please lady, just stop awhile and
Give time, to cast me a smile.

My tortured and agile mind cannot erase recent
Pleasant memories,
At your features and your face
I gaze in delight, my little legs prevent me from giving chase.

I guess there's a decade of years between us by far,
Age-a myth! Frustrated feelings, please give me time,
You move around so quickly 'lanky legs'! It turns me a little sickly

No time to spare, to ascertain, 'Am I your special friend?'
Who knows, who really cares, apart from me, so
Make me happy, to me be caring, do not drive me around the bend,

Because my dear, words can never say it all,
Especially if one's heart is smitten
And it does not matter what is written, as
Much has past and beyond recall.

D Robson

DRIVEN: UNFORGIVING

It wasn't spite that drove me. Vengeance, maybe.
Through piqued eyes, I see your other face,
Suffer corpulent harlot, for I have suffered for your,
Covert liaisons.
Openly you laughed at me. Spiteful, definitely.
Now my acrimony awakes, a grudge I harbour,
Stinging with malignancy, from my sedation I return to,
Even your treachery.
Quiet reflection on better times. Painful, obviously.
Unfazed by these memories, revenge is my fire,
Extreme and intense, the flames that once gave light
Now only burn you.
Clever attempts to appease my rage. Transparent, totally.
Everything told another lie, always a reason or alibi,
So flee from my ire, for it comes to destroy,
All you know and desire.
Liken my hunt to your worst fear. Frightening, hopefully.
Revenge is sweet, when it's mine I'll let go,
Menacing moments. Wonder. Wait. Hope. Pray. For
It wasn't spite that drove me. Retribution, possibly.

Jay Nicodous

AIN'T IT THE TRUTH?

You work like the clappers for your man and your kids
Wash hundreds of saucepans including the lids,
Hoover the carpets until they are bare
Whilst husband and kids just stand there and stare!
Then, in voices so loud you could hear them next door
They chorus together, 'Mum, can we have more cornflakes and
                                    toast and some marmalade please?'
Whilst I'm in the kitchen shelling the peas!
Get husband out of the door with a kiss
That ought to have been on my mouth but it missed,
It landed instead on the side of my face
As off to the station my husband did race.
Now get the children all ready for school
Sandwiches packed for each one, I'm no fool -
Butter one slice of bread, spread it with jam
Put down the baby outside in the pram
Collapse into armchair, totally shattered,
Wish there were someone to whom I really mattered
Maybe someday, just one of my crew -
Will say to me 'Mum - we couldn't do without you!'

Maisie Trussler

BEWARE OF THE CAT

The swallow's nest is building high
Just watch them flying in the sky
Getting ready for their newly born
But what's that I see on the lawn?

Oh no it's a dreaded cat
Well what about that
It sits there waiting to see
If it can catch a bird maybe

The birds have seen it so they take cover
Oh dear, oh no, here comes another
Two cats what will we do now?
We have to get rid of them somehow

There's a big dog next door
Maybe we could peck his paw
Perhaps it will make him bark, it might
Then hopefully the cats will run out of sight

Anything's worth a try isn't it?
Let's get the other birds to help, here's a blue tit
So the sparrow told the other birds what was occurring
And he thought he heard the cats purring

Suddenly there were birds flying everywhere
As they all made a noise around the dog that was there
Which of course this made the dog bark right loud
We'll get rid of those cats, the birds vowed

Yes, the cats ran away, that did the trick
Hurry, we must finish this nest right quick
Within the next day or two in the nest the baby sparrows lay
So for all the sparrows and their friends it was a happy day

Kathy Buckley

FOR YOU

For you I give my heart
A small offering then my soul
Will me to succeed when you fail
Many cry out in their pain

For you I walk the distance
Tread softly it is holy ground
Many are called, few chosen
Sing me a song of hope

For you I call out 'God'
Cry freedom, place a flower
Before the virgin's image
Cling to old memories rod of iron

For you I carry the cross
Some say you mean cross and passion
Lead on I will follow you everywhere
Fashion sets the pace we borrow the time

For you I have tasted the bitter cup
Swinging lady near a waterfall
Round or down, up and about
Memory has its own message

For you I gave up everything
Clothes, shoes from Harrods
The stuff dreams are made of
Take and sanctify all, for you

For you I hung against railings
Got my foot caught in a snare

S M Thompson

THE PHOTOGRAPHER

Smile please, say cheese,
All of us putting on a front for the happy couple
They oblivious of what's going on around them,
So much in love.
He, the forever pessimist standing aloof
Wondering how long it will be before bride and groom
Like most of the guests
Will be putting on a brave face to cover up
Their feelings.

Gladys C'Ailceta

SPRING UPON MOTHER EARTH

Spring is here no mistaking, our Mother Earth
Now turning all these vast shades of green.
Alas! These now forceful winds decreasing into a gentle breeze
Aiding our small birds to fly with much more ease.
So pleasing to see these little snowdrops appearing once again
Rearing up their tiny white heads supported with such vivid green stems
Bringing with them such joy and nostalgia of bygone springs.
Alongside, bluebells emerge like woven beds of shaded blue lace
Making one walk at a more leisurely pace
Enabling you to observe and value these first flowers of spring;
Not forgetting our animal kingdom, so mindful to come out of
Hibernation and inhabit once again on this now warmer Mother Earth
For here in the midst of all these new beginnings
Good shepherds are tending the birth of their new lambs bleating away -
Oh! this sounds so grand
Upon these fresh green pastures
A part of God's promised land.

Joyce Brown

FRED SWANSON

David was beaten up
by Tom, Tom gave
David a good thrashing
poor, poor, poor David
why do friends mainly
sometimes just fall out
for what unkind reasons
it's jealousy and fear
Tom said, David called
or said his mother
is fatter or bigger
than the Grand Canyon
Fred Swanson, David's dad
said Tom's mother tried
to attack him also
he said he was
going to go to
the police to report
the whole matter then
maybe see what could
be possibly done
then he smacked him
around the face hard
Fred Swanson, David's dad
said it's not right
it's just not on
Barnet has gone rough
also so very uncouth
with its rough persons

Richard Clewlow

MOON BENEATH THE SEA

The bed resembled a coffin inside a tomb,
Inviting the crumbled day whose hopes were slight;
I grab my pillow in the darkened room,
As the jaws of loneliness bite.

Caught up by its many lumps and pleats,
Like the hostile dunes of the desert sand;
Where, as an awkward giant I surveyed the sheets,
Entirely out of proportion upon uncharted land.

As the evening sun casts its final light,
From my weeping wounds I cower;
And from the terrors of the night,
When the acid minutes corrode every hour.

A train thundered past a quiet meadow,
And a grazing horse was suddenly startled;
It bolted towards an oak tree's shadow,
Where the whites of its eyes nervously sparkled.

When complex tunnels run deep underground,
Black windows have tiresome reflections;
There, forgotten moons are lost and never found,
And lights disentangle faces from their imperfections.

Many times, love and uncertainty caused my heart to quiver,
Now my expectations sink deeper than ever before;
Like a foundation stone was the gazing figure,
Supporting a house of oak, with sturdiness at its core.

Already knowing that permanence acquires an unshakeable beauty,
While transformation enjoys only a brief sense of purpose;
I understood the gallant moon had one regular duty,
To forge and echo shadows, fragile and nervous.

Martin Howard

FIELD OF CORN

Somewhere in the wilderness
My soul is resting and waiting
Belonging in a home
Invisible to the eye
Perhaps amongst the luscious trees
Or in the turbulent sky
I walk for miles and miles
But never to my home
I talk for hours and hours
But always feel alone
I am always tired but never worn
For one day the sun will shine
Upon my field of corn

Anna Moore

LONELINESS AND FEELING IT

L oving but lonely,
O n your own is lonely,
N o one to talk to is lonely,
E veryone will feel it in their life, being lonely.
L onely is unhappy,
I ndoors by yourself on Christmas Day is lonely,
N o one there to talk to is lonely,
E veryone will feel it in their life, being lonely.
S ad. Oh, loneliness.
S ad. Oh, it's lonely.

F earing to go outside,
E veryone feels it,
E veryone will feel it some day.
L oneliness. It's horrible.
I can't stand it. Loneliness.
N o, feeling only loneliness.
G loomy feelings,
S ad. Oh, it's lonely.

Lonely . . .

Alice Bithrey (9)

YOUR DREAMS I WILL SAVE

Release me my fair-headed one,
And let all the heartache be gone;
Fill all of your dreams
        With river and streams
And all of your winters with sun.

Release me my fair-headed girl,
Let all your emotions a whirl;
Fill all your desires
        With soft carolling choirs
And all of your hopes shall unfurl.

Release me, for I am your slave,
Within your commands I will bathe;
Make all of your words
        As sweet singing birds
And all of the things that you crave.

Marcus Tyler

THE LAKE

The lake rests still.
Calm. Serene. Clandestine.
Cloaked by a veneer,
its cool face unmoving.
Hushed as a nun bowed in prayer.

Wary? I endure! My thoughts unwritten.
Conscious of its glossy depth,
cryptic beneath the surface.
Hypnotic! It draws me in.
Parallel to that same lure
your eyes once held.

I chanced upon you strolling by its edge;
lost in April's seductive pause.
Your face reflected in the water's sheen
proved thoughtful. Distracted by
the trailing shadows of the trees
whose blossom's pink,
floated as confetti on the mirrored surface.

Was it true love? A passing phase?
A tale of fools mislead?
Caught in the web of summer's spell
my careless youth conspired against me.
Captive to your virile charm;
your savoir-faire:
I yielded without judgement.

Mystical beliefs embraced the past.
Conjured up phantoms:
Arthur! Guinevere!
Lancelot and Elaine.
And yet they spoke of perfidy.
Did history duplicate their story?
Was the legend of betrayal imitated in my eyes?

Now winter darkness sneaks in cruel - insidious!
Brittle leaves caress the lake;
they ride as fragile boats upon the dismal water.
The skeletal hands of the dying year
reach out in supplication.
Say their orisons. Wave a last goodbye.
As we two did:
Each to the other.

June Crosby Jackson

GWEN'S AMBITION

Gwendoline was sweet and twenty
Cutest girl in all the town
Suitors she had in plenty
But she always turned them down
For although her folks were humble
She herself was full of pride
And she cherished one ambition
To become a rich man's bride
Riches and a stately mansion
And of course a title too
Dancing, tennis and lots of travel
Nothing less would ever do
But as Gwendoline grew older
She began to change her mind
For she found a wealthy husband
Was very difficult to find
Days, and weeks, and months, soon faded
And her hopes faded too
If she couldn't share a mansion
Then she'd make a villa do
But when 'Mr Right' came later
'Cupid' laughed at Gwenny's plan
For she lost her heart completely
To a humble working man
Now she lives just for her dear ones
Time for idle dreams have passed
In an ivy-covered cottage
Gwendoline is rich at last.

D Hardwick

NOT LONG TO WAIT

Not long to wait before I call your name,
And you will look and smile at me,
Victory - for only you can turn
Each dream into reality
Endless nights I pray, that maybe someday,
Dark hours will be changed by you.
As long as you don't change, and as long as I'm the same,
No one can be unhappy with me and with you.
Do you ever wonder if we will ever be,
Be the same, when we are old?
As if we will change; we will be the same,
Be the same when we are old!
Because I don't know how long it will take,
You to be here with me,
All I know is that it will be hard,
Really; we need to be freed.
Ecstatic I feel, whenever I remember,
Each day that I spent with you.
Together we can handle any kind of problem - or
Each situation old or new.
Roam around the house as if,
No one lives here except me,
And I know the angels look out for us but, I am
Lonely and waiting for thee.

Sophia Shah

BRITISH HOLIDAY

To Southend in the summer
Many people flock,
To sunbathe on its beaches
And try its famous rock.

Mums and dads and little lads,
And aunts and uncles too,
All join in the fun and games -
It's like a blooming zoo.

And very soon they reach their digs -
(They have been there before);
Where a happy smiling hostess
Will greet them at the door.

And they quickly settle in,
It's just routine, you see;
A little bit of gossip,
And fish 'n' chips for tea.

And in the nice warm evenings
They stroll along the pier,
Or maybe find a cosy pub,
And have a glass of beer.

Or perhaps take in a concert
And greet their favourite stars,
And egg on blue comedians
With many ohhs and ahs.

The teenage members of the tribe
Sneak off on their own,
To seek out local talent
In the old familiar zone.

And when the week is over
They pack up all their gear,
Happy in the knowledge
They'll be back again - next year!

V B D'Wit

POT OF GOLD

I've got goblins up my garden
I know they are there for sure
I throw them little titbits
And the goblins come back for more

My cat knows there's something there
At night he will not stray
He will not wander up there
Not even during the day

They soon tell me
If something's wrong
I can hear their little voices
As they burst into song

They know I'm an old woman
That's getting very old
One day soon they will tell me
Where to find that pot of gold

Bert Booley

THE ADVENTURE OF LIVING

Despite its
Uncertainties
And
Obscurity,
Even
Through our
Disappointments
And mistakes -
The adventure
Of life
Leads us
Step by step,
From event to event,
From tragedy
To triumph.

Glenn Perry

MY LITTLE DOG

I sit here, by my nice warm fire,
With my little dog you see;
I listen to the stories
Winds down the chimney tell to me.

The window frame will rattle
My oil lamp light will dance
The fire sends out its shadows
Round my living room they prance.

My little dog, one eye shut
The other looking straight at me
I think he's saying go on mate
It's time to make a cup of tea.

I put the kettle on the hob
And from the fire there was a crack
It sent out one small orange spark
And hit my little dog Jack.

His ears went up, his tail went stiff
And he starts his noisy talk.
The silence broke, my quiet night gone,
I took him for his walk.

He's gone now, has my little friend
He was like a son to me
But he's still there by the fireside
When I make my cup of tea.

A F Mace

THANK YOU II

I hope you found your heaven
For mine holds no sunshine
I wonder if your face has changed
Because I would only notice
I let my memories unfold
And then feel envious of myself
I can see so much further
When I am looking back

Warren Brown

TUMBLING WORDS

I wonder where the words come from
Tumbling in my mind
Then suddenly they start to form
And even start to rhyme!

It seems a quite mysterious thing
And hard to understand
For as I write it seems sometimes
Not always by my hand

These words just flow along
Somehow, tumbling in my head
They nearly always seem to start
Just when I go to bed!

Happiness and rainbows and little furry cats,
With dear curly whiskers - teddy bears with hats
Lovely country gardens
With scents and sounds of bees
Stately silver birches - children on their knees
Picking tiny daisies - making daisy chains
Singing, shouting, happy, running home again

And still the words keep coming!
It's time I went to sleep
To give these tumbling words a rest
I'm sure they'll deeply keep

Joyce West

A Seat On The Board?

By stars, it seems, a life's ordained
For human, bee or gannet -
You, yourself, have no control
However you may 'plan it'.

So let us all accept our fate,
For nothing can retrain us,
It seems it all depends where God
At birth, did park 'Uranus'!

George A Tanner

VERY BAD WEEK

It's been a very bad week
Monday the bath sprang a leak
Tuesday my car broke down, the dog cut his paw
Wednesday I lost the key to the front door
Thursday I thought things were getting better
Then the post brought bills and a solicitor's letter
Friday the potatoes burnt that I put in to roast
Saturday the same thing happened to my slice of toast
Sunday the end of a very bad week
Is that water? I've got another leak

Malcolm Walker

MY NEIGHBOURS

(to the left)
A-L-C-O-H-O-L-I-C
is written on his thick, dry lips
I found out
that it is not any clear liquid
but a combination of Gordon's gin and tonic.

(to the right)
Every evening at six
They play Ella Fitz's J-A-Z-Z music
My mother-in-law wants to know why
They never ever get sick of it.

Lu-Ann Nicole See

DANGER

She walked along the garden path,
   Enjoying the sun and fresh air.
But all of a sudden, out of the blue,
   Something landed in her hair.

Glaring at the roof above,
   From which the missile was directed.
A huge fat seagull pranced about,
   Thinking it wouldn't be detected.

Its beady eyes met her stony glare,
   Then it cackled as it soared away.
As more of its friends settled on the roof,
   It was time to get out of the way.

M Wakefield

WHILST CHILDREN PLAY

Heat hugged sun, brood thunder's waiting gun,
Whilst children play, sheet lightning blinks the bay.
A sudden dark, beach clear, faster than the shark,
Cloud burst, a birth of teeming drops,
Seek cover in the shops.
Sandcastles slacked, run, spattered Union Jacks.
Another day begun, the little builders come.
All spades to hand, mushroom silver hillocks in the sand.
No thunderstorm, or tide, will shake their pride.
Hoist tattered flag, devote to fill a moat
Halt time, delay, the day,
To be a child at play.

A E Doney

A SMALL BOY'S LAMENT

I don't like abroad
And I'm terribly loud
When they don't understand what I say
The smell of their drains
And the noise of their trains
Are more than I'd stand for a day.

I showed them some snaps
Of Joey our Dachs
But they don't understand about dogs
All pets make them yawn
From the day they are born,
Those Spaniards and Ities and frogs.

I don't like their money
It's terribly funny
I never know how much to pay,
When I want an ice-cream
And I show them our Queen
They tell me to take her away.

The milk is all boiled
And the food is all oiled
And the water is dangerous to drink
I'm tired of Swiss flowers,
And Giotto's old towers
And sea that is as smooth as a rink.

What I like is Cornwall
It's so jolly normal
And they do understand what I say;
I can talk to the lads
And other boys' dads
And play in the pools all day

Next summer I won't go to Spain
I don't mind the wind and the rain
Or the sand in my ears and my shoes
I'll have donuts for tea
Where the bathing's all free
If only they say I can choose.

Phoebe Timpson

GIRLS ON BOYS

'Teacher! Teacher!
Brian Stim,
Thinks I like him,
But he's always covered in mud,
And always looks like a spud.
Teacher! Teacher!' says the girl.

'Teacher! Teacher!
Are you listening?
Brian Stim is sickening!
He just ate loads of figs,
And now he looks like a pig.
Teacher! Teacher!' says the girl.

Well, now ten years later,
I've heard word,
That Brian and her are lovebirds.

'Mother! Mother!
What shall I wear?
Brian's taking me out somewhere.
Why he's changed so much,
That I tingle every time we touch.
Mother! Mother!' says the older girl.

'Mother! Mother!
Oh he's so mature,
Why he's nothing like before,
Except for that gel,
Which makes me feel like hell.
Mother! Mother!' says the older girl.

Well it's amazing how boys change,
As we can see from your experience,
Alicia Strange.

Pooja Goel

YEAR 2000

The year 2000 is here at last
The stock market hasn't crashed
Planes are flying in the sky
Trains still running on electric lines
Banks were open, dead on time
Our cash is safe, so all is fine
We thank the experts, for a job well done
So let's party, have some fun
Now I don't wish to sound a jerk
Or be unkind for meek mirth
But isn't it time we all took stock
Admit, with Mother Earth, we'll run amock
So let's beware in this millennium
Realise, the creator of heaven, earth may come
And he will judge us one by one.

Elizabeth Grant

THE VISITOR

Wait a minute! What is that noise? The humming grew and grew
And there before us in the dark the object came into view.
It hovered there a moment more and then to our surprise
A beam came down to lift us up and take us for a ride.

The fear of flight did not occur as the aliens took our hands,
'Come with us,' they said, 'we will show you all our lands.'
The ship took off with the speed of light, and the earth
                                        beneath grew small
Time stood still as we hit warp speed, and the craft turned like a ball.

The world beyond came into sight and we landed on the sand.
Pyramids rose in the distance and temples ruled the land.
'They are just like ours,' we said. Then the memories seemed to fade.
'We built yours too, long before your humanity came of age.

We came to visit long ago, to help you on the road.
But your progress fell beside the way when we left to go abroad.'
'Where are we now,' we asked, 'in the past or future yet to come?'
'We are your past' they said, 'and your future has just begun.

We need your help this time round, our race is growing small.'
We smiled and nodded at each other, for they were only three foot tall.
Their leader came and took my hand, 'We come in peace,' he said
'No harm will come if you lie with me, our minds they need to meld.'

We lay down together on the sand, his cool hands touched my face.
Memories came flooding back of his time with the human race.
Tall and proud they stood long ago before the devastation.
Then war and nuclear holocaust had brought down their degradation.

Their fields and crops were all laid waste, but to their technology
they clung on
In the hope that one day soon a land they'd find with humanity
and a son.
Their future now lay in our hands, a small price to pay it seems
To relive our past, their present and then our future dreams.

The ship took us home, he waved farewell, to thank me he smiled.
When the time is right I will return, for you and our new-born child.

Sheila Storr

A PADDLE IN THE SEA

Our day is fine and very exciting,
The sea is a deep blue, and very inviting,
Over fine sands of a golden beach,
With a long way to go, the sea edge to reach.

Les has turned 70, game for a laugh,
Although a bit worried for an untimely bath.
Kathleen's a bit older, and bad on her pins
Needs use of a stick and Les' arm, for her sins!

You've got the picture, as off we stride
'You'd do much better, if you had a ride.'
'Not us! Never! Hold your hat on tight
For the wind is strong - as we're blown like a kite.'

We totter and stumble - as many laughs we hear
From Les's Margaret and my George, we hold so dear
Not far to go. Let's toss a pebble
Keep them waiting as we dibble and dabble.

What happened next? We are full of mirth
Both now sitting in two feet of cold surf.
For this wave came suddenly, angry and cold -
And we just succumbed, being brave and bold.

We are soaked right through, down to the skin
But we can't stop laughing, our bet we did win.
It was for us to have, in the sea, a paddle
With feet maybe - or what sits on a saddle!

Kathleen Aldridge

BROTHER

Brother, I still remember, when we were five or six
We would play at soldiers, our guns, of course were sticks
In our game of make-believe I would fall, and cry!
And you would comfort me and say, I won't let you die
Not knowing, that fate, would make that scene come true
And that one day for real we'd be soldiers, me and you
Young men, in uniform, for battle we were dressed
We were off to fight the foe, our heroism test
But this was not a game, our guns were real, not toys
Far removed from yesterday when we were only boys
My brother firmly shook my hand, and looked me in the eye
And said, 'If you stay by me, I will get you by'
To the front line we were sent, where bombs around us fell
We looked at one another and swore that this was hell!
It would take a miracle to see us through this night
As we fought, we prayed, that we would see the morning light
When sunrise came, I found you hurt, with wounds upon your head
Your body lying still, I cried, thinking you were dead
Then you turned and asked why I'd hurt you as we played
I hoped that what I heard, was no more than shock delayed
But you were badly hurt and would never be the same
A boy, trapped inside a man, that way you would remain.

Karl Jakobsen

A BIRD IN A TREE

One morning I saw a bird in a tree
It fixed its beady eyes on me
It seemed to be saying 'Put out some food,
'Cause I've got to feed a hungry brood.'
What could I do but respond to this plea
So I shared my breakfast with a bird in a tree
I divided lunch and dinner too
And over the weeks, those baby birds grew
Until one morning, I saw a bird in a tree
Now accompanied by the whole family
All grown up and ready to eat
Whatever I chose to throw at their feet
For days I continued until the cupboards were bare
With not a morsel or crumb left to be had anywhere
Impatiently, the birds started to tap on the windowpane
'Where's our food, where's our food?' over and over again
Morning and night they kept up this refrain
And the monotonous beat near drove me insane
Until, suddenly, I was blinded by a brilliant idea
And from that day forth, year after year
Those birds never came near my garden after that
Because I went and got myself a pussy cat!

Dino Carlin

WHO'S THAT?

Phew! Here's a little story I've got to do I'll tell of you. Fancy
getting through a window like you did, at the speed of sound you
ran and hid oh! yes you did. What have you done because you really
are one. Last I saw of you in the tree as I sat I the garden eating cake
and drinking tea, I could feel your eyes on me all the while, inside my
heart a wide smile.

With mountains to climb along with time to find to leave the time
behind and the future in the present. I can still see the feathers fly
fancy trying it on with a pheasant at times you are unpleasant
most of the time heaven sent.

P M Richards

WRITING FOR PLEASURE

Something to fill my lonely hours
Something to pass the time of day
Gone are physical things of enjoyment
Like gardening, walking or taking part in play.

So time to settle with a book to read
To think or meditate on an inner self
Calmer days, relaxed and at home
Sketching, painting or a 'chat on the phone'.

Once there was noise of children around
Days when one could not call 'their own'
Now in the tranquil, twilight years found
Reflecting happy days, as I sit alone.

Vicky Childs

A NEW REALM

He hit our dog,
Ploughed on,
Bumper dented
Carrying death's song
And left life's severed cord
Of ruby-red
To spill its ribbon
From crumpled crown,
Heart slowing down
Beating for its life
And death beating the
Beat
On the skin of a dying drum;
Crippled body my lame hands rest
And gently grasping time,
Mimic unspoken
Words
Cannot help the culprit fled
Left you in a dying bed,
So burst the fountain of salty waves
From the sorrow of my skull;
Your coffin a silhouette
In blind sight
Too small to absorb the prowess
Of your bones
Your life groans on the ebb and
Slumbers
Into the hands that
Speak
Gentle words in a new realm

Patricia A Thompson

THE BLIZZARD

It's cold, it snows, the east wind blows
I'm frozen stiff and red my nose
Frost is clinging to my clothes

I can barely see eyes shut as sleep
The snow was falling fast and deep
I could barely tread my feet

I cannot find which way to go
I'm all alone in storms of snow
I cling to fences, my pace is slow

What'll I do if I run out of fence
That will teach me to have more sense
Out in this blizzard the fog so dense

I'm shivering to the marrowed bone
Help me someone to get home
It was then I knew I was not alone

I felt a warmth within my heart
It leapt with quite a start
A light appeared thro' the dark

Have no fear, said a voice from the fog
Then I heard the bark of a dog
In my mind I prayed, thank you God

It's cold, it snows, the east wind blows
I'm frozen still and red my nose
Frost is clinging to my clothes

We three walked home together a little slow
Me, my dog, my wife who said, 'Not far now to go'
The joy gave me strength in this stormy snow

Oh! It's heaven as I stepped thro' the door
I almost collapsed upon the floor
I won't go out in a blizzard no more.

A Lawson

PINT-SIZE PENGUIN PETE

My name is Peter Penguin,
I am round and fat.
I've lots of fluffy feathers,
What do you think of that?
My friends all say I'm tiny,
I like to think I'm neat,
But they found me a nickname,
And it's 'Pint-size penguin Pete'.

I thought since I had feathers,
I would learn to fly,
I went out to the hillside,
To give it my best try.
I climbed up to the highest rock.
Stood on my tippy toes,
I climbed so high to learn to fly,
But I fell and bumped my nose.

I went down to the seaside,
With some friends of mine,
They didn't like the water,
But I thought it was fine.
I thought if I went down there,
I would surely drown,
Still I jumped in,
Now I can swim,
And I'm the happiest Pete in town.

My name is Peter Penguin,
I am round and fat,
I've lots of fluffy feathers
What do you think of that?
My friends all think I'm tiny,
I like to think I'm neat,
But they found me a nickname,
And it's 'Pint-size penguin Pete'.

P A Kelly

SHE WAITS FOR HIM

she sits alone
behind the locked door
waiting for him
but he doesn't come

she shouts, she screams
but her witch of an old mother
won't let anyone in
so she sits waiting
but he doesn't come

hush, she sleeps
the old woman,
a deep, drugged sleep
slumber softly, sleep
sh, he's coming

she unwinds her hair
a waterfall of gold
tumbles from the turret
sh, he's coming

Jean Buchanan

REBEL

Up garden path
Pass tall green grass
I hear bees buzzing
I see butterflies float gently by

Through the front door
Pass the longest hall
I hear footfalls
Belonging to my old good dog
I feel his head, nudge against my leg

Through the kitchen door
Out into the back yard
I feel my old good dog
Pass me, as he plays chase or football

Memories are all I have now
Since he died
Ten long years gone by

J M Stoles

MY WEE PAL

He was just
A tiny bundle
Of fluff and
Two blue eyes
But every day
He grew more
And in growing
Got more wise
At the table
He would wait
For titbits falling
Off my plate
He my companion
All the while
We would walk
Many a mile
But passing years
Take their toll
No more walks
Just gentle stroll
His little eyes
Seem to say
Time to go
I cannot stay
On my lap
Head he lay
Then he quietly
Passed away

Hazel V Wood

LOVE AT FIRST SIGHT

He walked across the room that night,
A neat figure of perfection.
   All dressed in black, with touch of white,
My gaze was in his direction.

   I wondered would he notice me,
As on the sofa sat I.
   With curler in hair and cup of tea,
Or would he pass me by?

   His eyes met mine and time stood still
As quietly on the sofa he sat.
   It really gave me such a thrill
To gaze at that handsome black cat!

Patricia Jeanne Hale

MOLLY

There once was a cat called Molly,
Who lived in an old shopping trolley.
Her bed was made from a dusty coal sack,
The rain kept out by an old plastic mac.
In spring she liked to eat the grass and flowers,
Go out for walks for hours and hours.
In summer she liked to stretch out in the sun
Lazing about, having lots of fun.
Every day she wound her way round people's feet
Hoping they would offer her something good to eat.
In autumn she liked to chase all the leaves,
Making the most of the last light eve's.
In winter she liked to stay out of the cold
Avoiding the frost, the damp and the mould.
But Molly had found one little friend,
This poem does not have such a sad end.
It was her dream to find a nice house,
To be a lap cat, chase the odd mouse
Get invited in, kept dry, a soft cosy seat,
A drop of milk, piece of fish, maybe some meat.
Young Olive would brush her black silken fur,
To be loved and looked after, it made Molly purr.

A J Chamberlain

PRIDE

All puffed up like a peacock,
Rubbing at it with a cloth,
His first car an old jalopy,
Face beams as he shows it off.

With rust spots on the paint work,
Minor things to repair,
It's my son's pride and joy,
Which he cleans with loving care.

A body kit he buys
And spruces up the wheels,
Weeks rubbing at its body,
Work for a re-spray he prepares.

A brilliant red custom car,
That's what it turns out to be,
Now when my son rides in it,
He's saying look at me.

All puffed up like a peacock,
Rubbing it with a cloth,
Face beaming full of pride,
As now he shows it off.

Helen Robertson

THE SANDWICH MAKER

Gowned and gloved, and masked like a surgeon,
Standing with knife held high,
'Is this my new job?' I say with a sigh!
I've joined the team, going down the line,
How did I know, that I'd have to keep in time.

Tomatoes, all sliced and cucumber too,
Ham and cheese to be weighed,
Stop one, butter one, drop one,
No time for the loo,
Says she who must be obeyed!

The conveyor belt has started,
Can you slow it down?
Hold on, it's going too fast!
As the sliced bread, goes racing past,
And you don't know, if it's white or brown!

Stop one, butter one, where did that slice go,
As the cucumber and lettuce go with the flow!
With butter at the ready, knife carefully poised above,
They discover I'm left-handed, and give me a shove!

At the end of the line, it ends up a soggy mess,
As the cucumber and tomatoes collide with the watercress,
The last man waits in a panic,
What's happened to his second slice?
Little does he know, I'm going frantic.

Does this one have cheese, does that one have pickle,
The girl standing next to me gives a giggle,
I'm never going to get used to this caper,
I think I'll go back to printing paper!

Anne Roberts

HIGH STREET ADVENTURE

It's many years ago now but I remember still
Of a time when I was young, I think I always will
When three of us teenagers were strolling through the town
Without a care and laughing as we were walking down
Towards the local golf course for a few friendly rounds
On that lovely day in June with all the summer's sounds
Suddenly a policeman appeared before our eyes
Held up his hand stopping us greatly to our surprise
'Can you spare a half hour lads?' he asked in a kindly tone
'Down at the police station, it should not take too long'
So we accompanied him and met there many more
Soon we were placed in line wondering what's in store
A prisoner was brought out and placed in the line
Two policemen then led out a young girl bearing signs
Of having been badly beaten up, her eyes were shiny black
The three went down the line and slowly walked back
On the return she stopped, near to me she placed
Her hand on the shoulder of the next man she faced
In distress she was led away they also took the man
They thanked us for our time, shook our hands, then we ran
Outside the sun was shining and our fears began to fade
But I will never forget that identity parade.

T Daley

THE HOSPITAL CHAPEL

With her face averted from
The stranger's gaze
She sat so still in the
Hospital chapel;

Sad, heavy thoughts
Bowed her shoulders down
Dark tired hair hid
Her cheek

Now she lifts a hand
To brush her cheek,
Did a tear fall there?
Dear God I hope not!

Michael Rowson

FULFILMENT OF A DREAM

In our youth we would dream that one day we'd be
Living together down by the sea.
A little white cottage right by the shore
Would be perfection, of that we were sure.
Gathering driftwood brought in by the tide,
Watching it burn as we sit side by side.
A stroll in the evening down on the sand
Watching the waves as we walk hand in hand.

We've lived in the country, we've lived in the town,
Worked in the city, moving around.
And all the time we were longing to be
In the bracing fresh air down by the sea.
Now we're retired, our dreams have come true,
We live on the cliff top, the sun shining through.
There through our window a glimpse of the sea,
E'er changing its moods, like you and like me.

One day it's silver as the sun gleams above
On clear days it's blue, the colour we love.
At times it looks grey, blending into the sky
It then disappears with mists swirling by.
No more in the country, no more in the town,
Done with the city, but staying around
Here in the place we were longing to be
Enjoying the beauty down by the sea.

Of course we're now old and hobble around,
But peace in our haven here we have found.
We witness God's power, His glory we see,
No man can harness the might of the sea.

Beryl R Daintree

A Cautionary Tale

This is the tale of Patricia May
Deaths and misfortunes made her day
At bus stops she gossiped of other folks' ails
Couldn't wait to repeat their sad tales.
Repetition enhanced them
Sympathetic smile on her face
She greedily recounted them
Any time, any place.

Arthritis was old hat, flu just a joke
Top of her list, heart trouble and stroke
Funerals she loved, anybody's would do
Something to talk of at length to the queue
I love a big send off
She would say with a smile
Cremations were too short
Not quite her style.

She choked on a fish bone
While eating some plaice
Lay there in the coffin
Rictus grin on her face
Friends and neighbours filed by
Two by two
'Doesn't she look happy
She loved a good do'.

Adrianne Jones

KISSES

Slowly you turn and lean towards me
I sense your aura as gently you kiss my cheek
A fleeting wisp moist and warm

Peacefully gazing at me
I taste your tongue as it delicately explores my mouth
A sensual comforting fresh cream eclair

Lightly lying warmly against me
I see your hands caress me as you suckle my breasts
Ever-changing like waves lapping the shore

Venturing in the twilight to my very being
I hear you moan as you eagerly kiss me and satisfy your hunger
With the juices that make me a woman.

Moira H Thorburn

THE CIRCLE OF LOVE

Two bodies separate
At the beginning of
Their time, but as they grow
Older their paths are sure
To meet, merge together
In unexpected ways
From their brief meeting at
College, to the crashing
Of their cars (her fault of
Course!) to the meal to say
She was sorry, the drink
To say thanks for the meal
From him, the moving in
Of flats, the mortgage, the
Wedding, the two lovely
Children, the three happy
Grandchildren, and then, just
As unexpectedly
Their bodies were torn in
Two, for their souls to be
Reunited in a
Different world and their
Love, friendship and trust will
Continue forever
They are soulmates and meant
To be together from
Now until the end of
Time - so let it be.

Lindsey Brown

MY BLUE GARDEN SHED

My garden shed is blue
And creaks and groans
Under the weight of odds and ends
I cram my dreams inside
That wait to see the light
Crazy messages I send.

I get lost in the blue
But always land on my feet
As in my shed I potter
I mould and I shape
It is my means of escape
The dream is getting hotter.

My garden shed is blue
And feels a little off colour
Cos it should have been green
It is a statement I made
Painted in deep blue shades,
A shed that must be seen
To be believed.

Ian Barton

THE DRESS

The dress was in the window of the little shop in town,
The model looked so haughty, as she displayed the gown,
The young girl stopped and gazed upon the style draped on the form,
And yearned to have it for her own (she'd come back in the morn).

The price was quite enormous, more than she could e'er afford.
She juggled her expenses of her lodgings and her board
And finally she thought that she could save a pound or two,
And with money carefully handled, this decided she would do.

She had a pretty little box she hid inside her drawer,
She put some coppers in each week, and wished that it were more
Each day she walked past by the shop, each day her heart would beat!
And sometimes she would float past, with wings upon her feet!

Oh, days of days! Oh, blessed time! She'd saved enough to buy!
She hurried down into the town and felt that she could fly,
The door bell jangled noisily, she, trembling went inside
And told the girl assistant, who listened and complied.

She counted out her money, and the dress was folded neat
And packed into a glossy bag she carried to the street,
She ran with jubilation to make her way back home,
She couldn't wait to get there and try the garment on!

She put up her umbrella to shield her from the rain,
The ground beneath her slippery, as she crossed the busy lane,
She didn't see the motor car which came upon her fast,
She went down limp and lifeless, with the bag still in her grasp.

The people milled around her form and sadly did their part,
They took the bag from out her hand and laid it on her heart,
They put her on a stretcher bare, and waved away the crowd,
They placed her in a coffin rare, the dress became her shroud.

Barbara J Settle

A STYLISH VOGUE

A genteel accessory the fan did adorn,
Along with satin gloves were worn.
A sumptuous party the ladies attending
To hostess with graceful curtsies bending.

These beautiful fans - their gowns to match,
Even held to disguise a patch.
Could show displeasure with imperious twirl
An elegant style in mother-of-pearl.

Waving the fan to create a stir,
Intention of being noticed by 'Sir'.
Peeped o'er the top with smiling eyes
A young man's fancy - the fan beguiled.

An invitation to join the dance,
Gladly received with modest glance.
Then whispers in corners - a promise to seal,
Behind the fan - a kiss to steal -

Fans with sequins and spangles were sewn,
With fancy lace edging trimmed to tone.
Held by a silken tasselled cord,
The most expensive one could afford.

Joy M Jordan

FLUFFY PUPPY, SCRUFFY PUPPY

Fluffy puppy, scruffy puppy
Wakes up in his bed.
Sleepy deep blue eyes
Peer from his baby head.

Fluffy puppy, scruffy puppy
Rolls around on the floor.
Jumps up at big brother
When he comes in through the door.

Fluffy puppy, scruffy puppy
Wags his tiny tail.
Leaps up with excitement
When the postman brings the mail.

Fluffy puppy, scruffy puppy
Chases his red ball.
Loses all his balance
And so skids along the hall.

Fluffy puppy, scruffy puppy
Snuffles in his bowl.
Naughty, playful, friendly pup
Uncoils the toilet roll.

Fluffy puppy, scruffy puppy
At the end of day,
Has worn out little paws
And no longer wants to play.

Fluffy puppy, scruffy puppy
Ready for a nap,
Curls up and falls asleep
Upon a cosy lap.

Lauren Pritchard-Gordon

VANISHING DREAMS

Seated on a bench in a park
having little to do with the day,
a woman, handsome, relaxed,
sits down on the other end.

In the distance a great metal bird
climbs above the rooftops,
screaming at the air,
carrying its payload onwards.

On no evidence my hopes rise;
the world is a brighter place.

She smiles as she catches my eye.
My brain pounds to form
words into coherent utterance.

The bird soars towards the blue,
engines throbbing strong.

My mind conjures dreams from nothing.
'Nice day,' I say.

The bird floats across an azure sky.
My dreams become wishes for a lifetime.

'Is it?' she says and, rising, leaves.

The plane vanishes into a cloud.
It begins to rain
and my fantasies turn to dust.

David W Lankshear

SOMEWHERE ALONG FUTURE'S ROAD

Along future's road you travelled, towards
your destiny that fate had written on your
brow, destiny mapped the way, the sorrows,
the joys, life, took you by the hand and
led you away. Somewhere along future's
road we'll be together again.

Somewhere along future's road, I know you are
waiting on me, fate and destiny are not to
know, life left it too late, to bring you to
me, yet in my heart I know somewhere along
future's road we'll be together again.

Somewhere along future's road, we'll stroll
arm in arm, happy at last, our hearts in tune,
in love again, singing happy songs of love
your tender and loving touch I'll know again.
Somewhere along future's road, we'll be together again.

Somewhere along future's road your eyes will look
into mine again, I'll see your warm loving smile,
I'll hear that wonderful voice again, I miss so
much, destiny I'm sure will lead me true. Here
on earth below, at the end of future's road
we'll be together again.

The Western Dreamer

EVERY POEM TELLS A STORY

Every poem tells a story, a story which must be forever told from love and distant places to clouds and daffodils that float upon the mind of man as each poem is unfolded from its beginning to its very end we hope these poems will never really end for poems tell a story, a story to behold from love and distant places to clouds and daffodils that float upon the minds of man as every poem tells a story, a story which must be forever told.

Michael Spittles

OLD TOM

They came to do a recce
Before the feature planned
Cameras, men and big feet upon our treasured land.
They promised it must be agreed
Whatever they had in mind
An 'historical record that must not be left behind'.

A farm house filled with treasures
Proudly on display
And photos of brothers and uncles long gone on their way.
This proud and eloquent farmer
Bemused by the presence of the crew
This attention meant for others, the prerogative of a few.

Then there was Daisy, Mo and Florence
And numerous other cows
Who knew not of modernisation
But the foreman's touch and sound.

They cared not that they were nuggets
Of bygone times and ways
And shots and cuts and edits
As their hand-milking was displayed.

The dog lay over barrel
Ear cocked at each sight and sound
Chickens ran free at leisure
And pecked nimbly on the ground.

The farm, yes, quite decrepit
Barely profitable any more
But tended lovingly for generations
Per the family motto over door.

'Of greed and profit you beware
Think of animal welfare'.

Gloria Hargreaves

MIDNIGHT DELIGHT

There's an old stone Teddy in the rockery in my garden
And he starts to wake when people go to sleep,
When the moon shines on the pathway and the flowers,
When the fairies meet and hedgehogs come to peep,
Ted stretches his fat legs and joins the fairy ring, to chat with
                                    elves and pixies,
To laugh and rhyme and sing.

One night whilst they were dancing, came an unexpected guest,
The witch from Barnswood Hollow, dressed in her midnight best.
A gown of black and rainbow, with golden moon and stars,
A hat of deepest darkness, a book of spells,
And jars of strangest colours,
A wand, a large black cat, a purse of precious stardust - now what
D'you think of that?

There was a secret meeting, I don't know what was said,
But when I awoke next morning, there was stardust by my bed.
And later in my garden, I found unexpectedly,
Some snowdrops - (out of season),
It was their gift to me!

Irene Moor

RAGS TO RICHES

My mother and father were as poor as church mice
And each day that came brought struggle and strife
My mum looked haggard and her eyes were dim
And I've promised myself I'll be a rich man's wife

I've grown into a woman now
And blossomed into a beauty
I'm starting work at the big old house
And to Mum and Dad I'll do my duty

I'm scrubbing floors and washing clothes
My poor hands are red and sore
But I am getting five shillings a week
My mum will be happy for sure

The master has summoned me, he wants a word
I've done nothing wrong, oh what can it be?
He beckons me to sit down on a chair
Then he asks me if I want to be his daughter's nanny

And now I am dressed in dresses of silk
I've said goodbye to my poor humble life
And the promise I made all those years ago
Has come true, for I'm to become his wife

E A Lilley

IT'S A MUG'S LIFE

I began life as a clay ball in a pottery kiln
All discomfort and heat just one among many
Neither handsome or smart my future pre-set
No doubt my life span a short one, if any!

With luck I might have been reasonably fashioned
Commemorating with pride some Royal event
To live on as a relic of times that were passed
And not just forgotten, a souvenir 'Present from Kent'

Thus into the world I emerged pristine and clean
To suffer in silence whatever my short life brings
Including rough handling without thought or care
Stained with vile liquids and all manner of things

I survived for some years with many a near miss
It was all too good to last as I realised full well
As I lay finally shattered just a few bits on the floor
My life summarily ended by a child's plaintive yell

I couldn't help it Mum, it just fell out of my hand!

'It's a mug's life alright - bloody kids!'

M F Base

A Bargain At The Boot Sale

If you spare me a moment I will tell you a tale
Of the day we went to the car boot sale
Little trailers and vans seemed to sprout everywhere
Eagerly waiting to sell us their ware
Trestles and tables had all taken root
Colourful carpets spilled from out of a boot
Odd bits and bobs, old curiosities
Tables piled high with silly atrocities
There were rusty old tools and bright flowerpots
Bundled together as 'separate lots'
A stall bedecked with china pigs
Curling tongs and 'fashion' wigs
Knitting wool and crochet hooks
Collections of cassettes and books
We traipsed 'round the field and had so much fun
Finding something or other to please everyone
Then we came to the end, thought we'd seen every stall
When one of our party espied near the wall
A table so tiny, its surface quite bare
Just an old fashioned lamp and a picture stood there
The fellow in charge said 'Please make a bid'
And I laughingly said 'I'll give you two quid'
Home with my picture I happily went
Pleased with myself and the two pounds I'd spent
A faded old photo in a dusty old frame
But a wonderful bargain for me just the same
For I carefully cleaned it, and got such a start
It turned out to be quite a fine work of art!
My little oil painting admired by all
Now takes pride of place from a hook in the hall.

Barbara Davies

'HOUSE' BINGO

How I love my dear old bingo,
It's fun to go and hear the lingo,
I'd love to shout out 'House' sometime,
But sadly it's over; I rush for the door.

I get outside, it's very dark
Cars are parked all around the park
Somehow I fall and hit my head,
I'm spread out on the pavement, nearly half dead.

People all around me, keeping me still,
All bringing an ambulance, for me to fill,
Off to hospital I'm whisked away,
No more bingo, for many a day.

Pulled ligaments, muscles and nerves, no broken bones,
Takes longer to heal, more painful, with plenty of moans,
Months and months of staying at home,
No more to my dear bingo could I roam.

Then all was coming back to life,
I walked again, there was no more strife,
It seemed as though, through all the dark days,
My wish for bingo again would be a haze.

But then someone did ask me out,
They took me to bingo, and I did shout,
House! House! I kept on repeating,
My day had dawned and I wasn't sleeping.

Now my bingo days are back again,
But no more slip ups, I'm careful, no more pain
To ever keep me from my favourite game,
The 'bingo' kid, I'll always remain.

Phyllis Wright

DOUBLE TROUBLE

At home we have a cat called George,
you can see where he's been, by his muddy paws.
His coat is coloured white and black,
he eats and sleeps all day, he's a lazy cat.
If you want to see him move really fast,
try to spray him and he will rocket past.
Last year he went missing, for quite a while,
we thought he'd just gone out on the tile.
Then one day, my son was riding his bike,
when he saw a cat by the roadside, that looked alike.
I went with my son to look at the cat,
hoping it wasn't ours and that he'd come back.
But I couldn't tell if he was ours,
he had been run over and had been dead for hours.
We carried him home anyway,
and I said I'd bury him later that day.
I took him to the woods, opposite our house,
where he used to go, to catch a mouse.
I dug a deep hole, by an oak tree,
I was blubbing now, and hoped no one could see.
'Goodbye Georgey boy,' I said,
'you were my favourite cat and I'm sorry you're dead.'
I steeled myself and walked back from the wood,
we would all miss him, and I did what I could.
As I put my spade back inside the shed
something rubbed against my leg.
It was George! I could hardly believe my eyes,
the cat I had buried, was the same colour and size.
Welcome back Georgey boy, you old wag,
it's good to see you, you old flea bag.

Colin Dudley

TOMB OF FATE

As we sit in the darkness,
In the cold and the damp,
We think of that night,
That miserable night.

As the rain poured down,
And the mud swelled,
Around our feet,
We trudged forever onwards.

Not daring to look back,
Never daring to admit,
We were lost,
Trudging aimlessly forward.

Only one thing certain in our minds,
That the battle was lost.
We saw comrades slaughtered,
As we ran, made our escape.

But our fate,
We knew not.
Until we entered,
That tomb of death.

It was hopeless to fight,
But we still fought on.
We watched men drop, so many,
We had to give up.

And now we sit in this cell,
Awaiting our death.
We remember friends,
They died with us, for us.

And now in the darkness,
I listen and wait.

Alan Harrison

THE TEASING MAGPIE

A family of five magpies
Came into the garden one day
They ate the bread spread on the grass
Then flew into the apple tree
When one young bird started to play.

A black cat walking near the garden fence
The magpie did espy,
To the fence he flew and landed on a post
Close enough to catch the black cat's eye.
The black cat went into offence
He hunched his back, his fur stood on end,
Snarling he jumped up at the post
Where the magpie waited and seemed to laugh
At the last moment he flew to the next post.

Cat followed by jumping to the ground
At the post he jumped up, magpie was not around
Back to the first post he had flown
This game went on for quiet a while
The cat got bored and walked away.

Magpie got daring and jumped to the ground
He did not see the other cat, which had come around
But the watchful magpies in the tree
Attacked the cat,
Making sure the young bird flew free.

Irene Pierce

NEAR TO HEAVEN

I was on a plane journey
Not so long ago
Flying way up in the clouds
So pretty like snow
When my dear little granddaughter
Then only four
Looked out of the window
So deeply in thought
'Do you know Nana,' she said
Her head in her hand
'Must be near to heaven
This white fluffy land
Because we are higher
We've not been before'
How sweet and quite true
From a child only four

Jeanette Gaffney

TEARS OF A BROKEN HEART

Teardrops fall just like the rain
From a young girl's broken heart.
And she could not understand why
She and her man fell apart.

In the beginning life was so good
And each day was a real pleasure.
When he said that his love was true,
She thought she'd found her treasure.

But then he became so distant
And the lies poured thick and fast.
Before she knew what was happening,
The present became the past.

Then, there was the telephone calls
In the middle of the night.
When the other girl quickly hung up,
Tears of pain clouded her sight.

And when she asked him about it,
He said she was just being paranoid.
From then on, their romance died
And her heart was null and void.

One day, while going through his washing,
She found the perfumed love letter.
And the passionate words she read
In its pages, truly upset her.

She confronted him with it later
And a violent row ensued.
She cried alone on her bed all night,
Now fully aware she had been used.

In the morning when she woke up,
She discovered he had gone.
She knew her heart had been broken
And the love no longer shone.

She couldn't come to terms with it
And felt decidedly ill.
She arranged her clothes neatly on
The bed, and swallowed the final pill.

Peter Steele

HOME IN THE WOODLAND 1941

The year is 1941
Eight boys and girls are on the run
Is there to be an invasion?
We prepare to overcome.

A visit to a nearby woodland gave the clue
A tree house we would build.
All through the holidays we disappear
From morn to night we toil.

Our parents never worried.
Two hours British summer time gave us light.
No rape or murder in those days,
We were safe as safe could be.

A thick ear at home - if our trousers were torn,
Nought to worry Mum anymore.

At last our tree house is complete.
No one would know we were there.
If the invaders came - we would be safe.
Safe in the woods of Birchcliffe Edge Bank.

Janet Cavill

THE ADVENTURE OF A WATER DROPLET

'I don't want to let go,' said the droplet on the tree.
'Oh do come down and run with me,' said the sparkling stream
'I glide out to the sea.'
With a trickle and plop the water droplet dropped,
and with a splash it joined the stream.
Over the stones it rippled and all the little fishes tickled.
How pleased I am that I let go and fell into the stream below.
Now into the sea I will flow.
'Come on my friends still clinging to the tree
let go and come with me to the gigantic sea, and with me be
free to ripple and flow.
Then all around the world we will go.'

Patricia M Farbrother

OVAL AND OGLE?

Our rugby team brings home a cup, on each face a smile, no frown,
A team of men with their heads held high, bringing honour to our town.
A group of men in defence, the danger of being attacked,
Cheered along by supported cries, in the stands many fans are packed.
Once again the hallowed turf produces a winning team,
Alas, the lads have returned home with a cup, no longer is it a dream.

John P Evans

Goin' Fishin'

There was a young fellow called Mike,
Who set out after school to catch pike;
First he hooked an old shoe,
Which caused quite a to-do;
Then his line got caught up on a spike.

So he took off his shoes and his socks,
And he bashed his bare toes on the rocks;
But he freed his line,
Which then did entwine
Round some flowers in a window box.

He cast once again without care,
And the window box sailed through the air
To land with a crash,
And a deafening splash
In the river which flowed past just there.

A woman was passing who saw
The commotion and said, 'Oh my Lor';
If a coffin it ain't!'
Then she came over faint,
And fell flat on her face on the floor.

This action so frightened poor Mike,
He packed up and set off on his bike.
With the day almost past,
He pedalled home fast;
So he never did catch his pike.

Aw, shame!

Roger Williams

SIX MICE

Six mice went looking for food
Along the skirting board
They came across a piece of cheese
Wrapped in a piece of wood

First mouse said 'I'll take a bite'
Opening his mouth quite wide
The others looked with bated breath
As he disappeared inside

Five mice went looking for food
Behind the pantry door
They came across a piece of cake
That had fallen on the floor

'I'll try it first,' said number two
Silly was his name
He took one bite and fell asleep
Never to wake again

Four mice went looking for food
Under the kitchen mat
Alas they found no crumbs at all
Just a great big ginger cat

Three frightened mice turned and said
'We're wise although we're small'
And single filed into their hole
We're not hungry after all

Georgina Waite

HECTIC!

'Where's my lipstick?' asked Mum
'No - not that one - it's the wrong colour!'
One eye on the weather
As it grew duller

She looked in the mirror
'I'll wear a hairnet to go in
Then it'll be alright
When I'm out there goalin'!'

She searched for nail varnish
Then she asked for her clean sweater
Then she decided that
The other one was better

'Where's she going?' you may ask
'To the dance of her dreams?'
No - she plays today
In the ladies' football team.

Choosing mascara and
Checking if her shorts still fit her
She found - 'They don't do a
Thing for my figure!'

Then exclaimed she - 'Oh no -
I've got a pimple on my face!'
She gave up - and gladly
Dad went in her place.

Barbara Sherlow

LONELY NO MORE

Roses grow on a lonely hill.
The birds and trees are oh so still.
Just a little cross marks one grave.
Nothing left! Nothing to save.
A lonely child was buried there.
When alone and ragged people did stare.

Now little one, you are not on your own.
Where there was a heart, is now a stone.
The sun will shine for where you rest.
Flowers will bloom at their best.
Sleep little one from dawn to dusk.
For now in our Lord's Heaven, rest you must.

No more ragged clothes for you to wear
No more dirty a face for people to stare.
Rest, sweet one, for in Heaven you'll be.
No more the worry for the world to see.

Janett Carol Hardy-Pierce

L'EAU DE VIE

All my air castles
Have melted like snow
And their waters
Run down to the quarry below.

Then succulent colours
Stop one to admire
A glint in the pool
Of life you require.

As moments in time
Ebb and flow
A breeze floats around you
With nowhere to go.

A feast of surfaces
Play on the eyes
For nature's elements
Have no demise.

A curtain call
Is not for the making
But a new episode
There for the taking.

Your moment is eternal
A smile from eye to eye
Goodbye is not a word I know
'See you around!' is what I utter - as I go.

A S Pugh

GREAT SKELLIG

Off shore - deep in South West Kerry
Once was developed - monastic life
Isolated - bleak - alone.
Upon top of a craggy barren outcrop
Standing as though in pontification
A humble dwelling was borne.

Painstakingly built - centuries ago
By monks - a brotherhood in scorn.
Carving out a meek existence
While from mankind's bosom - torn.
Yet being at one with the elements
Coexisting in a humble state - forlorn.

But nowadays their position's extinct
Claimed only by lighthouse - bird sanctuary
And nature reserve - adorned.

Precipitous rock once more embodied
Tourism off Bolus Head - reborn.
With purpose inexplicable restored
- Indestructibly stubborn.

Gary J Finlay

CASUALTIES

Julie,
Russell,
Paul,
and me.
A class situation,
Or crime scene?

Outlines of four,
dusted,
chalked:
spread-eagled,
entwined,
on a carpeted floor.

Objects remained,
of what went before,
while gun shapes,
pointed,
their target,
ignored.

A naked bulb
illuminated these . . .
remnants,
of an evening.
We left,
relieved.

Amy Phillips